Best Tips And Tricks For Soap Making

Time Honored Soap Making Techniques

By: Sandy Chase

TABLE OF CONTENTS

PUBLISHERS NOTES

Disclaimer

This publication is intended to provide helpful and informative material. It is not intended to diagnose, treat, cure, or prevent any health problem or condition, nor is intended to replace the advice of a physician. No action should be taken solely on the contents of this book. Always consult your physician or qualified health-care professional on any matters regarding your health and before adopting any suggestions in this book or drawing inferences from it.

The author and publisher specifically disclaim all responsibility for any liability, loss or risk, personal or otherwise, which is incurred as a consequence, directly or indirectly, from the use or application of any contents of this book.

Any and all product names referenced within this book are the trademarks of their respective owners. None of these owners have sponsored, authorized, endorsed, or approved this book.

Always read all information provided by the manufacturers' product labels before using their products. The author and publisher are not responsible for claims made by manufacturers.

© **2013**

Manufactured in the United States of America

DEDICATION

This book is dedicated to my aunt who taught me the secrets to making great homemade soaps.

CHAPTER 1- WHAT IS SOAP MAKING AND HOW DOES IT WORK?

The art of making soap has existed for hundreds of years, and for the majority of that time, soap was made by hand. If you wanted soap, you saved the necessary components from daily life and made it yourself. It wasn't until the 1920s that soap became a commercial product, bought rather than made. In the last decade or so, the art of making soap has seen the resurgence among eco-friendly people. Thankfully, while the chemical process behind making soap is complex, the physical process is not.

The History of Soap Making

The oldest known mention of soap is actually over 4,000 years old, coming from ancient Babylon. The recipe for a simple soap, consisting of ashes, alkali salt and water was written on a stone tablet dated to around 2200 BCE.

One popular tale of the discovery of soap comes from ancient Rome. In Latin, the word that means soap is Sapo. As the tale goes, there once was a mountain named Mount Sapo. This mountain was a frequently used site for animal sacrifices, and thus became saturated with animal fat over the years. One day, particularly heavy rains washed the animal fats down towards the river, alongside ashes from the sacrificial fires. These three ingredients -- fat, ash and water -- are the primary ingredients for basic soap. Washerwomen at the banks of the river discovered that the refuse from the mountain cleaned clothes much more easily than water alone, and named the substance Sapo.

This tale, while interesting, is almost certainly not true. There is no record of a mount Sapo anywhere in the Roman Empire. There is also little evidence that soap was used as a detergent in Rome, as it is rarely mentioned in any capacity.

No matter the history, the basic recipe stays the same, though today we use more refined products than animal fat and wood ash.

The Methods of Making Soap

All natural soaps -- those not created with synthetic detergents -- are made with three primary ingredients. The first, water, has remained unchanged since time began. The second, animal fat has been replaced in modern times with various vegetable oils. Home soap makers often choose a mixture of olive and coconut oils. The third, ash, has also been replaced with the active ingredient from that ash. This ingredient is caustic soda, or lye.

There are three ways to make soap today, though one of them is more of a craft hobby than an actual soap making process.

Cold Process: This method is the one used throughout the ages. You mix a proportion of lye with water in one container. In another container, you mix the oils you will use. Then you combine the two ingredients, stir, pour into molds and let it set. The lye and the oil react in a process called saponification, chemically transforming into soap. The chemical reaction takes a significant amount of time, so the curing process takes six or more weeks for a batch of soap.

Hot Process: This is similar to cold process, though it is a much more modern invention. Rather than mix the ingredients and let them sit for weeks, you mix them over a source of heat close to boiling. This forces the chemical reaction to progress faster, curing a batch in hours instead of weeks. For proper results, this requires constant stirring and is not recommended without plenty of time to dedicate to the task. Once the soap has been poured into molds and cooled, it is ready to use.

Melt and Pour: This process is more of a craft hobby than a soap making method. Instead of working with oil and lye, you buy unscented clear soap base. This pre-processed soap works as it is.

Melt this soap and add your preferred colors and scents pour it into molds and allow it to set. You now have soap.

The Saponification Process

Saponification is the technical name for the chemical process that produces soap. It begins with the fatty acids found in animal fats and vegetable oils. When these fats are introduced to a sufficient amount of a strong alkaline element, they react. This reaction produces soap.

Two different kinds of alkaline are commonly used in making soap. Sodium hydroxide is the biggest player, which produces a hard bar of soap when introduced to oil. Potassium hydroxide is a more recent chemical, which produces liquid soap instead.

The saponification process works beyond the basic oil and lye reaction. In fact, wet chemical fire extinguishers operate on the same principle. Grease fires burn much hotter than liquid fires, so the standard fire extinguisher will not work. Wet chemical extinguishers spray the necessary chemicals that will cause saponification in the grease, which does two things. First, it reacts with the grease, turning it into a non-flammable soap. Second, the chemical reaction itself absorbs heat, reducing the ability of further grease to flare up.

Interestingly, saponification is not always a good thing. In the art world, oil paintings are at risk of saponification, a process that has been observed around the world and in paintings from all time periods and geographic locations. The fatty acids in the oil paints may react with heavy metals and alkaline compounds in the pigments or in foreign contamination, causing saponification.

Though the ingredients have changed, the art of making soap endures through the centuries. No doubt, people will still make soap by hand for centuries to come..

CHAPTER 2- SOAP MAKING METHODS EXPLAINED

Making soap, while initially complicated, quickly becomes a matter of experimentation and adapting recipes. Once you're involved in it as a hobby, you can easily turn it into a small-scale home business. Before you can make it that far, however, you need to know the different methods for making soap. There are essentially four primary ways to make soap.

Melt and Pour

Melt and pour soap making is the easiest and safest way to make soap. You do not need to handle dangerous lye, monitor mixing temperatures or worry about exact measurements. However, melt and pour soap making is not quite making soap. It is more like re-purposing soap.

With the melt and pour method, you first need bars of existing soap. You can use slivers of leftover soap from your own purchases, or you can buy large blocks of clear, odorless base soap. The first step is to melt this soap base. You can do this over a double boiler or simply in the microwave, it is that safe and easy.

The fun of melt and pour soap making is what you do with the melted base. While the soap base is hot and liquid, you add your additives. A few drops of fragrance oil will give your soap base a nice, refreshing scent. You can also add color using any of the FDA-approved soap colorants.

Once the soap has been colored and scented, simply pour the liquid into a mold. You can use anything from plain block molds to ornate patterns. You can get creative with layers of different colors, artfully mixed swirls and combinations of scents.

Melt and pour is by far the easiest and safest method of making soap. It's a great hobby, it can lead to a productive business and it's perfectly safe for children. Try it out at a school activity, make soap for holiday gifts or do anything you want with the soap you make.

Cold Process

Cold process soap making is the old-fashioned method used for hundreds of years. This is where chemistry comes into play, as well as potentially hazardous chemicals. Before you start trying to make cold process soap, make sure you have the proper gear and equipment. You need eye protection, rubber gloves and lye-resistant tools.

The original soaps were made using ash and tallow, but in modern times soap makers use vegetable oils and lye. Lye comes in two varieties, sodium and potassium, each with different uses. Potassium hydroxide is used for liquid soaps, while sodium is used for hard bar soaps.

Your choice of oil is limited to organic, non-petroleum oils. Coconut and olive oils are the most common, but you can add in hemp oil, cocoa butter, Shea butter or any other oil you want. Just make sure you learn the saponification index of the oils you use, so you know how much lye you need to add.

The actual cold process involves mixing the right proportions of lye and water in one bowl, and mixing the desired oils in another. You then mix the two containers and allow the mixture to react. Depending on the size of the batch, this takes a long time, with the usual process taking six weeks or more to cure completely.

Cold process soap is scented and colored in much the same way as melt and pour soaps. You add certain fragrance or essential oils to the process and these oils add scents to the finished soap. Dyes and certain powders, such as cinnamon and paprika, can be added to soap to give it color. You can even alter the texture of the soap.

Certain oils add moisturizing qualities to the finished product, while additives like pumice or oatmeal give it a rough, exfoliating quality.

As with melt and pour, cold process soap is formed in molds, usually in large blocks. You can carve it or form it in other molds as you desire, though you need to be aware of the settling that occurs if you use particulate additives like oatmeal.

Hot Process

The hot process is very similar to cold process soap making. Rather than carefully mix the ingredients and allow it to cure over weeks, you instead mix all of the ingredients and bring it to a boil over a heat source. As you stir the mixture, it will react with the oil and lye while evaporating excess water.

Hot process soap is more high-maintenance, as you need to continually stir the mixture until it has fully reacted. Once the reaction is complete and you remove it from the heat, you can allow it to cool and harden in molds. Once the soap is cold and hard, it is ready to use. This means it takes much less time than cold process soap. Hot process is a relatively new procedure, but it is growing more popular in recent years.

Re-batching

Re-batching soap is also called French or Triple Milled. It is, essentially, adding another step to the cold process procedure. You follow the same process as cold process soap -- hot process works as well -- and allow the soap to harden. With hard bars, you then grate the soap into slivers and heat it with a little water. This melts the mixture and allows you to add more color and scent to the soap.

The benefit of triple milled soap is that the standard process often degrades the scent oils somewhat, or breaks down other additives that give the soap moisturizing and healing properties. By re-batching, you are able to preserve these qualities.

Chapter 3- What Ingredients Are Needed For Making Soap?

All soaps are based on three ingredients. These three ingredients are water, oil and a caustic agent such as lye. Within this framework, there are dozens of possible ingredients, as well as a wide range of additives to give your soap color, scent and other benefits.

Oil

The oil you use depends on what is most readily available to you. The best oils for old-style soaps are animal fats, such as lard and tallow. Unfortunately, these oils are difficult to acquire in sufficiently large quantities. Most soap makers today use vegetable oils. The best oils to use are coconut, palm, soy and olive oils, in various proportions. These oils are most likely to result in a firm, hard bar that still lathers quite well.

Petroleum-based oils do not work for soap. These include petroleum itself and products like mineral oil.

Additionally, you can use specialty oils in much smaller quantities to add some side benefit to your soap. For example, adding almond oil, hemp oil, castor oil, cocoa butter and Shea butter have various moisturizing and creaming effects. They will make your soap creamier and will add their own faint scents to the mixture.

Caustic

The lye additive is essential to soap making. Without it, you will simply have an oily bar. The reaction of lye and oil, called saponification, is what produces the soap itself.

There are two types of lye primarily used in soap making. These are Potassium Hydroxide and Sodium Hydroxide. Each has its own purpose, and which you choose depends on the kind of soap you wish to make. Potassium Hydroxide will make a liquid soap when it reacts with the oil. Sodium Hydroxide will create a hard bar of soap. If you wish a cream or lotion-style soap, you will need to mix them in various proportions.

The lye reacts completely with the oil during the soap making process. The final product will not actually contain any lye, so it is safe to use on skin. Caustic lye is dangerous to handle on skin, so the reaction is necessary.

Water

Believe it or not, the water you use has an important effect as well. You can use distilled or filtered water for good effect. Alternatively, tap water is possible, but you need to be aware of the chemicals that are added to standard tap water. Generally, if using tap water, you will want to let it sit for a day or two before using it. This allows certain chemicals, such as chlorine, to evaporate off the water. For a more naturalistic soap, you can use collected rainwater. The natural minerals will add a slight organic benefit to the soap.

Scents

Scent is added to soap using additional oils. You will use either essential oils or fragrance oils. Typically, if you are making soap on a commercial scale for sale online or at a farmer's market, you will make a variety of different scents of soap. A solid mixture of different oils will give your soap a distinct smell, which is primarily what attracts people to a given variety of soap.

Essential oils are natural oils that come from plants. For some types of scent, such as pine or vanilla, you can harvest and produce your own essential oils. They are also relatively cheap to purchase from a scent oil supplier. Some essential oils, however, are prohibitively expensive. Rose essential oil, for example, can cost upwards of $3,000 for 16 ounces, because it takes over a ton of rose petals to produce. Experiment with essential oils and you can produce a wide range of scents just by varying proportions and ingredients slightly.

Fragrance oils are the other end of the spectrum. They are artificially produced and cannot easily be made at home. Some of them are scent blends that include some essential oil, while others are completely artificial. The term "nature identical compounds" comes up in this industry as well. These are laboratory-produced chemicals that have the same molecular structure -- and thus the same scent and properties -- as natural essential oils. Most floral scents are artificially produced for the same reason as the rose example above, while most food-type scents -- coffee, chocolate, mango -- are artificial from the start.

Coloring

Changing the color of soap requires an additive or dye. Some powder additives are introduced for their effects on the soap, such as cinnamon or paprika, and will change the color of the soap as a side effect. Most colors, however, are added with a simple dye.

Before using a dye in soap, you must make sure it is on the Food and Drug Administration list of approved colorants. Many dyes are not approved for use on skin, or in sensitive areas such as lips or eyes. This limits the available number of colors you can use. However, the soap industry is large enough that any color may be produced with the right combination of dyes. As a soap maker, however, some people may simply prefer an uncolored natural soap. This allows you to skip an ingredient altogether.

Additional Additives

Adding oatmeal to an organic soap is an easy way to include an exfoliating scrub. Adding jasmine or peppermint can give an additional cooling effect, as well as a mint scent that adds to other scents. Some ingredients can be added to increase later and for moisturizing effects.

Producing soap can be an enjoyable hobby, a lucrative business and anything in between. Experimenting with oils to develop the perfect soap scent and feel is all part of the fun.

Chapter 4- Ten Soap Making Recipes

Soap recipes vary from exceptionally simple, requiring only a few steps, to particularly difficult where many ingredients are required. Soap making goes beyond putting together the recipes; however, and today's homemade soaps often look like works of art.

Polka Dot Soap

This creative soap will look terrific in a modern bathroom and will also dress up the soap dish in the children's bathroom as well.

Ingredients

3 pounds "melt and pour" glycerin soap base
3 different liquid colorants (your choice of color, non-bleeding variety)
3 small bowls
Circular cookie cutter (about 1 inch)
Square silicone brownie pan

Directions

Create the dots by melting a small portion of the soap in one of the glass cups and then adding a few drops of the colorant into the mixture. Put the mixture into the brownie pan and allow mixture to harden. Take the colored sheet out of the pan and repeat the process for the other two colors. Cut dots out of each sheet with the circular cookie cutter. Then melt more soap and pour a thin layer of the melted soap into the brownie pan. Allow the soap to harden for a short time and then put a layer of dots down. Add more clear soap to the pan and put another layer of dots down. Then finally add the rest of the soap and allow the mixture to harden.

Tip: Spraying the surfaces with a bottle of rubbing alcohol reduces bubbles.

Olive Oil Soap

There are a few different ways to make olive oil soap and the result usually depends on what type of olive oil is used.

Ingredients

16 ounces water
6.5 ounces lye
5 ounces coconut oil
40 ounces olive oil
5 ounces palm oil

Directions

Since this is lye-based soap, it's more advanced, and all the standard materials will be required (cooking pots, measuring cups, ladles, etc). To make the soap, measure and melt the oils on the stove until they're around 100 degrees. Combine the lye and the water. Add the oils and the water together and use a stick blender to mix for about a minute. Pour the soap into a mold and allow it to cure in a warm place.

Blue Sugar Scrub Soap

This recipe makes small sugar-cube soaps that last just a single use, and which may also be made in other colors if the soap maker wishes.

Ingredients

2 ounces clear glycerin soap
2 ounces grape seed oil
6 ounces white sugar
Blue liquid colorant
Raspberry fragrance
Small square soap molds

Directions

Melt the clear soap and mix it with the grape seed oil. Add the blue colorant to the mixture and ensure it's thoroughly combined. Add the fragrance and mix again. Add the sugar and stir until it's well blended. Pour the mixture into the small square soap molds. Allow to harden.

Laundry Soap

Save money on detergent by making this simple soap for the laundry.

Ingredients

4 pounds of lard
8.4 ounces lye
20 ounces water
2 ounces of fragrance (optional and soap maker's choice)
Grater

Directions

Heat and mix the lye and water together. Melt the lard. Mix the heated lye mixture into the lard and then add fragrance. Pour the solution into the soap mold and allow it to harden for at least a day. Cut the soap into squares and after about a week, grate the soap for use as detergent.

Lemon Scented Soap

Lemon is a terrifically fresh scent for the bathroom. This wonderful recipe is simple and easy to make.

Ingredients

Goat's milk soap base
Lemon essential oil
Lemon zest (around 4 lemons)

Directions

Melt the soap base in the microwave. Stir in the essential oil and the zest. Pour into soap molds and allow the mixture to harden.

Chocolate Brownie Soap

This soap will smell just like a chocolate brownie, but remember that it's not edible!

Ingredients

6 ounces coconut oil
10 ounces olive oil
6 ounces distilled water
2.25 ounces lye
1 tablespoon castor oil
2 tablespoons unsweetened cocoa powder
Vanilla oil drops

Directions

Since this is lye-based soap, it's more advanced, and all the standard materials will be required (cooking pots, measuring cups, ladles, etc.). Measure and melt the oils on the stove and then combine the water and lye in a separate container. Mix the oils and the lye solution together until it's fully blended. Slowly mix in the cocoa powder and then add a few drops of vanilla. Pour the mixture into the soap mold and allow it to cure in a warm place.

Zucchini Soap

A zucchini-based soap is a terrific exfoliating agent, and this recipe is very simple to make.

Ingredients

2 pounds melt & pour soap
1 medium zucchini (pureed)
4 teaspoons rose hip oil
2 tablespoons vitamin E oil

Directions

Melt the soap and add the zucchini and oils. After the mixture is fully combined, pour the soap into molds and allow it to cure for about 3 days.

Vegan Soap

Many soap recipes require lard, and that means the soap isn't vegan. The following recipe is great for anyone who doesn't want to use animal products.

Ingredients

6 ounces water
1 ounce castor oil
4 ounces coconut oil
2 ounces olive oil
1 ounces sweet almond oil
1 ounce cocoa butter
7 ounces palm oil

2.2 ounces lye

Directions

Since this is lye-based soap, it's more advanced, and all the standard materials will be required (cooking pots, measuring cups, ladles, etc). Combine the water and lye in a single pan. Then combine all the oils together. Mix these components together and then stir in the cocoa butter. Pour the mixture into the soap molds and allow it to cure in a warm place.

Mini Soap Cubes

This cute recipe is a great way to make tiny, fun soaps for decorative purposes or for any sort of special occasion.

Ingredients

Clear glycerin soap base
Colorant (any color will do)
Ice cube trays

Directions

Melt the soap base in the microwave and when it's a liquid, add the colorant into the mixture. Pour the melted soap mixture into the ice cube trays and allow it to set for a few hours.

Simple White Soap

Everyone should know how to make basic, white soap. This simple recipe is a great option for beginners.

Ingredients

41 ounces cold water
14 ounces lye
74 ounces tallow
32 ounces vegetable oil
3 ounces cocoa butter

Directions

Heat and combine the lye and the water. Heat and combine the remaining ingredients. Stir the two batches together and then pour the final mixture into a soap mold. Allow it to harden for a few days.

Chapter 5 - How to Add Fragrances in Soap Making Recipes

One of the best parts about making your own soap is adding the scents. You can make your soap smell like anything you want. There are endless varieties of scents. The first step is to learn the process. Adding a smell to soap is not as simple as pouring in a perfume. You have to pick the correct oil and then add it at the exact right moment in the soap making process.

Ingredients

You will need to get either fragrance oil or an essential oil. These are the only things you can add that will give a powerful smell. You can't add perfumes or colognes. They will not hold the scent in the soap. Many first time soap makers are tempted to take their favorite perfume and pour it into their soap mixture. They then are upset when the soap doesn't smell anything like their perfume.

The reason you can't add a regular cologne or perfume is that you are adding it to the raw soap. The soap mixture has to be cured. In the liquid state it is still transforming. There is lye that has yet to be converted into soap. This means that the fragile chemical nature of the perfume will be destroyed by the soap.

What you need are oils that will bond with the soap. These oils are going to be called either fragrance oils or essential oils.

Fragrance oils are not made from real flowers or fruits. An example of fragrance oil would be Piña Colada or Almond Biscotti. These are made to smell like their namesakes but are made with chemicals. They cannot take a cookie and extract oil from it and add it to soap.

Fragrance oils are much cheaper than essential oils. They are safe for humans. Most soap and shampoo on the market uses fragrance oils.

Essential oils, on the other hand, are made from their namesake. Lavender essential oil is made by taking lavender and crushing it and extracting the oil. The same with something like Tea Tree oil or Lemon. It is possible to take lemon peel and extract the oil. That oil can then be added to the soap.

Many people prefer using essential oils because they have a much stronger smell. They will last longer in the soap. It is common to make lavender soap and have it retain its smell for several years. Many soap makers keep their soaps in their linen closets and notice that the ones made with essential oil have a wonderful long lasting scent.

How to Add the Fragrance to the Soap

Once you have selected the fragrance you want you have to add it to your soap. It is important that you understand at what point you add the scent. If you add it too soon you can destroy the oil and the soap will not have any smell.

The first step in making soap is to mix the lye with the water. This is harsh. You should never put the scent into this mixture. After you have mixed the water and lye you will add the main oil. If you were making olive oil soap, then the main oil would be olive oil.

After you add the main oil you will mix it. You want the mixture to get thick. Most people will use a stick blender. You can use a plastic mixing spoon but this will take a long time. It might take you up to twenty minutes using the blender and up to an hour using the hand spoon.

Once the soap mixture has gotten thick you will want to add the fragrance oil. You will pour the oil into the soap and then continue to mix it. You want to make sure that the oil gets evenly dispersed. If you don't mix the fragrance oil then you will be stuck with soap that does not have a consistent smell.

How Much Fragrance Should You Use?

Most soap makers will tell you that you should only use about 1 teaspoon per pound of soap. Once you have made a batch of soap you will see if the recipe needs to be adjusted. Sometimes you might find that the particular scent you choose is not powerful enough in the cured soap. If that is the case you can increase the amount of fragrance you add to the recipe.

Can You Mix Fragrance Oils?

Yes. Many people mix different oils in order to get a unique scent. Some popular combinations are Tea Tree Oil and Peppermint, Coconut and Lime, and Vanilla and Cinnamon.

If you are planning on mixing two oils together, then you only have to use half a teaspoon for each. There is no need to pour twice as much of the fragrance oil into the soap.

Can You Add Fragrance Without Adding Oil?

The simple answer is no. If you were to add Lavender leaves into soap it would not make the soap smell like lavender. The only way to get a soap to smell a certain way is to add the fragrance oils or essential oils we have spoken about.

There are some people who find that simple coconut oil soap will have a faint coconut smell. This is true if you use a really high quality coconut oil. However, the smell will not be very strong. If you want to make a really powerful coconut smell you will need to use coconut fragrance oil.

Chapter 6- Tips on Making Soaps – What Every Soap Maker Should Know

Making soap is at once an incredibly easy and a very complex process. It's easy because it only involves three basic ingredients: water, oil and lye. Its complex because each of the oils reacts differently to different types of lye, needs a different amount of water to react properly and may need different additives for different results. Here are several tips for every budding soap maker to make life easier.

Why Make Soap?

Making your own soap is easy once you have the tools and processes down. It's also quite inexpensive. The initial investment of oils and lye may cost more than a few bars of soap, but you can make an incredible amount of soap with those ingredients. You can use the soap yourself, or you can sell it at local farmers markets or over the Internet. In sufficient quantities, you can turn soap making into a lucrative home business. Soap making is also good for the environment. Homemade soaps lack the synthetic ingredients that come in commercial soaps. The most basic soap is made from a bit of ash and a bit of animal fat, both of which are highly natural ingredients.

Prepare, Prepare, Prepare

If you're cooking, you don't want to be halfway through the process before you realize you're missing a key ingredient. You also don't want to find out you're missing oven mitts when you need to pull a dish out of the oven. You need to prepare for any project, and soap making is perhaps more reliant on preparation than most. A mistake in the process can result in a lumpy, half-formed bar of soap that at best barely works, and at worst can be dangerous. Here are items you will need:

Protective gear: Rubber gloves and protective glasses are essential

Mixing bowls: Make sure your bowls will not react to lye, which means no thin plastic, aluminum or wood. Steel, glass and enamel bowls are ideal, preferably with lips for pouring.

Solid mixing implements and measuring spoons: At least one large mixing tool needs to be heat resistant, and at least one set of measuring cups needs to be non-reactive to lye. You might also consider an electric stick blender for the timesaving power it possesses.

Without an accurate scale for liquids, you cannot make soap reliably.

A way to measure the temperature of two hot liquids: This may be two solid, accurate candy thermometers, or it may be an IR laser thermometer.

Molds: The simplest molds are wooden boxes lined with waxed paper, or glass and steel molds. Once you have the process down, you can use fancier shaped molds.

Plenty of cleaning supplies -- rags, towels, etc -- to clean up spills. You will be working with oil and lye, both of which are difficult to clean up.

Learn About Lye

Lye comes in two forms: sodium hydroxide and potassium hydroxide. Sodium is used for solid bar soaps, while potassium is used for liquid soaps. Cream soaps use a mixture of the two. Lye also comes in many forms, from flakes to pellets to powder.

Lye is dangerous. Lye is a caustic chemical that burns skin, strips paint and eats away at fabric. Learn about lye before you start to use it. Learn how to protect yourself -- that's why safety glasses and rubber gloves are on the essential items list. Learn how to clean up spilled lye. Make sure you only work with lye in a ventilated area, as concentrated lye fumes can be dangerous.

If lye comes into contact with skin, use vinegar to neutralize it.

Before you begin measuring lye and oil to make soap, learn about the saponification process. This is the chemical reaction that makes lye and oil turn onto soap. Different oils require different amounts of lye to saponify fully, and you need to know these measurements before you begin.

Consider the Methods

There are several different methods for making soap. The most common is cold process, where you mix a water/lye mixture with oils and let it saponify. You can also use hot process, which does the same thing at a boiling point to cure the soap faster.

If the thought of using lye is intimidating, or you have a reason to avoid the chemical -- such as children in the house -- you can try melt and pour. Melt and pour takes existing bars of soap and melts them. While the soap is liquid, you can add your own scent oils and dyes to combine. Pour the melted soap into molds and let it cool. This is a fun way to make soap with children as a project. It is also a good way to use up leftover scraps of soap that otherwise melt or get thrown away.

Don't Be Afraid to Experiment

Once you have the basic process down, have a reference for different proportions of lye and oil and have a stock of ingredients, you can experiment. There are dozens of different oils you can add to soap to make scented soaps, both with natural essential oils and with artificial fragrance oils. You can also add certain dyes to color your soap. Creative use of scents can produce perfumes as interesting as any candle store.

You can also experiment with molds and colors to create interesting shapes and designs in your soap. This is more time consuming, but the result can be a beautiful piece of homemade soap that works well as a gift.

Once you've learned about the soap making process, it's easy to get started. It's a fun hobby when the proper safety precautions are taken, and it can become a wonderful business opportunity.

CHAPTER 7- HOW TO ADD DESIGNS TO SOAPS WHEN MAKING SOAP?

After learning the basics of making homemade soap, getting creative with designs, colors, and objects is a popular way to learn more about making personalized soaps. Just about any type of item can be placed inside a bar of soap, and the design ideas are only restricted by the soap maker's creativity. The easiest way to add designs into soap is to use the "melt & pour" style of making soap.

Adding Swirls into Soap

An advanced technique in soap making, creating swirls is an activity that might require some practice for the best results, but the nice thing is that even if the design is a little messed up, the soap is still usable, even if it turns out looking a little strange. It's also likely that some thought will need to be put into the colors used for a swirly soap, especially if it's meant as a gift for a certain occasion or person.

Ingredients

"Melt & pour" ingredients for white bar soap
"Melt & pour" ingredients for each color of soap for the swirl
Large soap mold capable of holding around 15 bars
Large soap divider
Spatula

Steps

Create batches in separate containers of white soap and each of the colored soaps
Add the swirl pattern of colors into the base of the soap mold (so the bottom has a design!)
Carefully pour the white soap on top of the base swirl design
Pour the top layer of swirls on the soap (long, curved lines work well)
Insert a spatula into the mold until it hits the bottom and drag it through the mold via the thin side
Insert a soap divider into the mold and allow the soap to harden as usual

Tip: For the best swirling results, make sure the consistency of each soap color is similar

Adding Objects into Soap

One of the most popular ways to dress up a plain bar of soap is to put an item (like a tiny rubber ducky) into the soap for fun. Holiday-themed items are terrific for soap gifted during Halloween or Christmas, and special items may also be placed inside soap meant as birthday gifts. As with other creative designs, using a "melt & pour" solution is often best for inserting objects into the soap. Consider also that an object doesn't need to be smaller than the final soap size. It's fine if part of the object sticks out of the side or out of the top as such a design can create a nice, artistic effect.

Ingredients

"Melt & pour" soap making ingredients
Small object (something plastic works well)
Soap mold in any size desired

Steps

Melt the soap solution
As with a regular bar of soap, add any color or scents desired
Pour a small amount of the soap into a mold
Position the item into the mold
Allow the soap to set for a few minutes
Add the rest of the soap to the mold

Allow the soap to harden and solidify

Adding Pictures into Soap

Adding a photograph or a picture into a bar of soap is a nice way to personalize the bars, and also opens up some very artistic avenues for creating fun soap. Anything from newspaper clippings to magazine pictures may be used, as well as photographs and even hand drawn pictures (hand crafted pictures should always be drawn with indelible ink).

Ingredients

Clear "melt & pour" soap making ingredients
Soap molds the size of each picture
Rubbing alcohol (in a spray bottle)
Pictures, photographs, or drawings for the soap

Steps

Melt the soap solution

Pour a short layer of the soap into the soap molds
Allow a few minutes of solidification of the soap
Spray some rubbing alcohol on soap
Immediately place the image (face down!) on the soap
Add the remaining soap solution to the mold
Allow the soap to harden

Tip: Some scents may change the color of a picture. Be careful when adding scents to soap that feature pictures.

Adding Words or Impressions to Soap

Inserting a word, name, or message into a bar of soap is a creative option for a gift and is also very easy as there are a few different methods available for adding words to soap. One of the easiest ways is to use "melt & pour" soap and to stamp the soap with a special soap stamp after it's already been hardened a very short time in the mold.

Ingredients

"Melt & pour" soap solution in any color
Soap molds in any shape or size desired
Soap stamps of shapes or words

Steps

Melt the soap solution
Pour the entire amount of soap into the molds
Allow the soap to harden only as long as it takes to hold its shape
Remove the stamps from the molds and depress stamps into the surface

Tip: The best results for stamping soap usually come from lye-based recipes. If all that is available is a "melt & pour" solution, adding some water to the mold should keep the bars soft enough for proper stamping.

The preceding projects aren't the only ways to add fun designs to soap, and each of these basic techniques may be refined over time as the technique for making the soap designs gets easier. It's also necessary to note that not all of these projects are simple the first time they're attempted. Purchasing enough ingredients to perform these projects a few times ensures that a few batches may be used as practice soaps so as to get the technique just right.

ABOUT THE AUTHOR

Sandy Chase tried her best to make as many changes to her own home to make it safe from anti-bacterial soaps; the level at which antibacterial soaps are being used in the average household makes this scenario a distinct possibility. The collective phobia that exists around bacteria has contributed to the development and subsequent popularity of new cleansers whose personal and environmental impact we've yet to gauge.

One of the most prominent of these is tricoslan, which can be found not only in soaps but also deodorants, mouthwashes, toothpastes and an increasing number of other consumer products. Its overuse could cause resistant strains of bacteria to develop. These, in turn, would rearrange the competitive hierarchy within their ecosystem. It is in everyone's best interest to learn how to make their own soap and the Best Tips and Tricks for Soap Making by Sandy is the perfect opportunity for this.

The FDA has considered restricting the use of antibacterial soaps because its panel of experts has not found them to be any more effective than regular soaps in combating infections. Traditional cleansers like soap and hot water, chlorine bleach, alcohol and hydrogen peroxide are all sufficient for the average household's sanitation needs. Most of the common diseases that we face are caused by viruses, anyhow, which are not destroyed by antibacterial products. Follow what Sandy the expert is teaching and make your family safe.

2699748R00029

Printed in Germany
by Amazon Distribution
GmbH, Leipzig